THE ROOTS OF
TOLKIEN'S
MIDDLE
EARTH

THE ROOTS OF TOLKIEN'S MIDDLE EARTH

ROBERT S. BLACKHAM

TEMPUS

Frontispiece: J.R.R. Tolkien photographed in his Oxford garden in 1966 by Pamela Chandler.

First published 2006

Tempus Publishing Limited
The Mill, Brimscombe Port,
Stroud, Gloucestershire, GL5 2QG

British Library Cataloguing in Publication Data.
A catalogue record for this book is available from the British Library.

ISBN 0 7524 3856 5

Origination by Tempus Publishing Limited
Printed and bound in Great Britain

Contents

Acknowledgements

This book could not have been written without frequent reference to a number of other books. These are the most thumbed and, in some cases, the most falling apart: *J.R.R. Tolkien, A Biography* by Humphrey Carpenter, *The Cole Valley South (The Millstream Way)* by John Morris Jones, *The Complete Guide to Middle-Earth* by Robert Foster and *Birmingham Pals* by Terry Carter.

I would also like to thank the following people: Andrew Butler for fine editing the text and making it more bookish, together with the Tolkien Society. The staff at Tempus for helping me to get this book published. Chris Upton for his 1992 Tolkien Discovery Trail guide that got me started on what was to become this book.

For help and support from my five local libraries: Birmingham Central Library's Local Studies and History, Hall Green, Acocks Green, King's Heath and Yardley Wood.

King's Heath Local History Society, Moseley School, Sarehole Mill Museum staff, the Volunteers of Moseley Bog and The Shire Country Park Rangers. The staff at Selly Manor Museum who have put up with me going on about Tolkien for years.

Local radio, national and local television stations who have brought me to a much wider audience. (I even appeared once as a Black Rider in a programme about healthy walking!)

I also thank all the people who have come on my guided walks and helped me see places through other's eyes and everyone who has helped me in other ways to produce this book.

Finally, thanks to my family for all their support and help over the years that it has taken to produce this book.

Preface

For many years, and especially since the success of the film adaptations of J.R.R. Tolkien's most famous book, *The Lord of the Rings*, there seems to be a sort of 'Queen Elizabeth slept here' mania, with all sorts of places with more or less tenuous connections to the famous author making extravagant claims about where he stayed or got the inspiration for some of his detailed and vivid descriptions. Fortunately, however, the Birmingham area, where Tolkien spent his formative childhood years, is now getting more of the attention it deserves and, as you will see as you progress through this book, Robert Blackham has done the research to back up his claims and found images to illustrate the points he makes.

Whether you can make the trip to explore Middle-earth (or, at least, Middle England) for yourself or just want to see it from the comfort of your own armchair, this book will prove invaluable.

The Tolkien Society, founded by Vera Chapman in 1969 to further interest in the life and works of J.R.R. Tolkien, CBE, the author of *The Hobbit*, *The Lord of the Rings* and other works of fiction and philological study, is proud to have Robert as a member and a work such as this adding to the scholarship on our favourite author.

Andrew Butler and Ian Collier
March 2006

The Tolkien Society

Based in the United Kingdom and registered as an independent, non-profit making charity, the Society boasts an international membership in over forty countries. The Society helps to bring together those with like minds, both formally and informally, with gatherings locally and nationally throughout the year. Recently we have been involved in weekend events in May based at Sarehole Mill and the setting up of The Shire Country Park and we are continuing to work with other groups in the area on other Tolkien-related projects.

Our three main events at national level are: the Annual General Meeting and Dinner, held in the spring in a different town or city in the UK each year; the Seminar, which takes place in the summer and presents a programme of talks on a Tolkien-related subject; and Oxonmoot, held over a weekend in September in an Oxford College, with a range of activities such as talks, discussions, slide-shows and a costume party.

The Society produces two publications: the bulletin, *Amon Hen*, appears six times a year, with Tolkien-related reviews, news, letters, artwork and articles, both humorous and serious; the annual journal, *Mallorn*, is more serious in nature, with longer critical articles, reviews and essays.

Within the Society there are local groups spread throughout Britain and the world called 'Smials' (after hobbit homes). Here both members and non-members can gather to discuss Tolkien's works, as well as other writers and topics. The formality and seriousness of meetings varies depending on the members. In addition to these there are also Special Interest Groups, covering topics such as collecting, biography and Tolkien's languages. For young members there is an active group, 'Entings', which has its own section in the Society bulletin.

The Society has a website, which provides members and non-members with general information about itself and the world of Tolkien: http://www.tolkiensociety.org

The Tolkien Society
Hon. Pres.: the late Professor J.R.R Tolkien. CBE *In Perpetuo*
Hon. Vice Pres.: Priscilla Tolkien
Founded in 1969 by Vera Chapman

Registered Charity N°. 273809

For further details please write to:

The Secretary (BBAB)
210 Prestbury Road
Cheltenham
GL52 3ER
United Kingdom

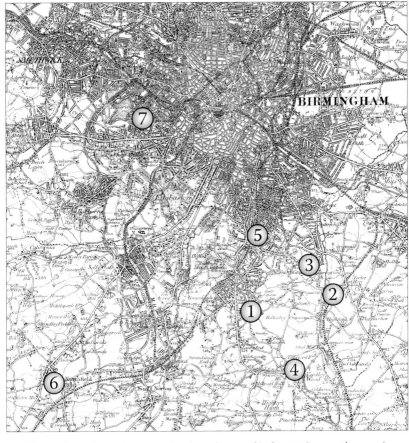

Birmingham city centre, central and south, 1905. (Ordnance Survey, sheet 165)

① King's Heath

② Sarehole

③ Spring Hill College

④ Titterford

⑤ Moseley

⑥ Bristol Road to Rednal

⑦ Edgbaston Reservoir

Introduction

.R.R. Tolkien lived for much of his early life in and around the British industrial city of Birmingham, but he was born in Bloemfontein in the Orange Free State in southern Africa in 1892. Both his parents, Arthur and Mabel, had moved there from the Birmingham area and married in Cape Town in 1891. This book is not a story of his life, as others have already covered this. It is a snapshot of some of the places that led to the development of the books, *The Hobbit* and *The Lord of the Rings,* set in the fictional world of Middle-earth. These books, written later in his life while living in Oxford, were destined to change English literature in the later part of the twentieth century and into the twenty-first century. They have spawned a vast world of fantasy fiction such as that represented by *Harry Potter*, *DiscWorld* and *Star Wars* and on into the world of computer games. *The Lord of the Rings* has been voted people's favourite book in a series of polls: in the UK, from a Waterstones/Channel 4 survey in 1996 to the BBC's 'Big Read' in 2003 and elsewhere, including Germany's ZDF TV 'Das große Lesen' in 2004 and the international 'Millennium Poll' in 1999 on Amazon.com.

In a recent estimate, *The Hobbit* had sold around 75 million copies and *The Lord of the Rings* over 100 million worldwide, and has been translated into thirty-eight languages. With the release of the *Lord of the Rings* films – *The Fellowship of the Ring* (2001), *The Two Towers* (2002) and *The Return of the King* (2003) – millions more all over the world have discovered Tolkien's fictional world of Hobbits, Elves, Dwarves, Orcs, Dragons, Wizards and Men. It is amazing to think that in recreating Tolkien's fictional worlds on film New Line Cinema went 12,000 miles from England to New Zealand and probably used more computing power than a space agency to produce what Tolkien must have seen in his mind's eye when he was writing the books.

Birmingham may appear to be a strange place for the roots of some of the greatest fantasy works of the twentieth century, but, with its industrial heart and sleepy rural surroundings, all within a short walk or tram-ride of each another, this area did play an important part in the creation of Middle-earth. The time period of Tolkien's early life was one of great change: it began in late Victorian times and moved through the Edwardian period to finish in the great tragedy of the First World War and the Battle of the Somme, in which Tolkien and many of his school friends fought.

The city of Birmingham in the early 1900s was full of people from all over the world and had steam-driven trams, trains and engines and levels of pollution that we could only imagine in our worst nightmares. The rural edges of Birmingham, in the counties of Worcestershire and Warwickshire, had horse-drawn carts and ploughs, blacksmiths' shops, watermills, timber-framed buildings and meadows full of wild flowers.

In a rare interview in 1966, reproduced in *The Guardian* newspaper in 1991, Tolkien described how important the little hamlet of Sarehole on the rural edge of Birmingham had been in the development of his fictional vision: *It was a kind of lost paradise... There was an old mill that really did grind corn with two millers, a great big pond with swans on it, a sandpit, a wonderful dell with flowers, a few old-fashioned village houses and, further away, a stream with another mill...* Further on in the article he re-emphasizes the importance of his childhood memories of the area: *'I could draw you a map of every inch of it. I loved it with an (intense) love... I was brought up in considerable poverty, but I was happy running about in that country. I took the idea of the Hobbits from the village people and children...'*

This idea of a simple life was very much to Tolkien's liking and when writing about the heroes of the books, the Hobbits, he said: *'for they love peace and quiet and good tilled earth: a well-ordered and well-farmed countryside was their favourite haunt. They do not and did not understand or like machines more complicated than a forge-bellows, a water mill, or a handloom, though they were skilful with tools'.* This is on the very first page of the Prologue to *The Lord of the Rings* written many years after his childhood days in the little hamlet of Sarehole on the edge of Birmingham.

Some of these places exist today and are like walking through one of Tolkien's manuscripts; one or two of the pages are missing and some of the pages are at other locations, but by a miracle much has survived to this day.

I was born and lived in the River Cole Valley in Birmingham and played in many of the same places that Tolkien had played in as a small child. In the mid-1990s I thought that someone should do something to celebrate the fact that Tolkien had lived in Birmingham and I started doing some research. This was the start of a journey that was to lead to the creation of this book, although I didn't know it at the time. I wrote a tour guide called *A Journey Through the Old Forest and Shire* and started taking groups of people on guided walks. Then one day I was 'phoned up by journalist Charisse Ede of the *Birmingham Post* newspaper and asked what I thought about New Line Cinema making three films of *The Lord of the Rings*. To cut a long story short, she came on the walk with me and wrote a great piece on it in the paper. This led to more people coming on the walks and some radio and television appearances. A little later on I started giving talks about Tolkien and Birmingham to local groups, as I still do today. This raised small sums of money which I used to buy postcards of the places that had connections with Tolkien and his books from his time in Birmingham; where possible postcards that came from the Victorian and Edwardian periods. Collecting the postcards has taken a number of years and has meant looking at literally tens of thousands of postcards. I have met some very helpful people at postcard fairs.

The modern photographs have, in most cases, been taken from areas that are open to the general public, but I have also been able to visit a number of sites not normally accessible. If you do come to the Birmingham area to follow some of the trails do please respect people's privacy and property. Tolkien himself suffered later in life as people invaded his garden in Oxford trying to photograph him through the windows of his house in the 1960s.

Other places and events, of course, also played their part in Tolkien's fictional world but places and people from his time in Birmingham are scattered throughout the pages of his writing. This book sets out to show the reader the world of Tolkien's early life in and around Birmingham and how this was to re-emerge in his later life when creating the fictional world of Middle-earth.

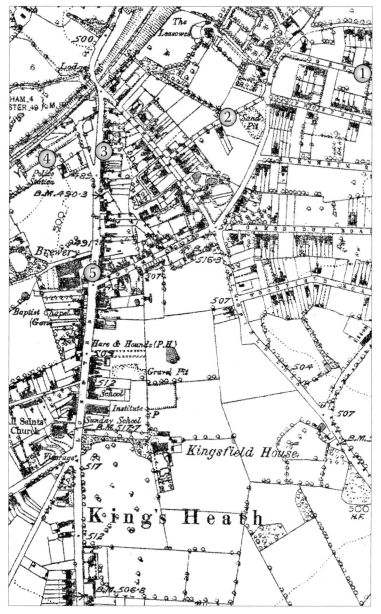

King's Heath, 1882. (Ordnance Survey. Worcestershire sheet X1 NW, Warwickshire X1X NW)

1. Green Hill Road
2. Ashfield Road
3. The Station public house
4. King's Heath railway station
5. King's Heath High Street

Chapter 1

King's Heath

The journey or story starts in 1895 when Mabel Tolkien returned from Bloemfontein to visit her parents in the now leafy suburb of King's Heath. At that time King's Heath was not yet a part of the city of Birmingham, but would become so early in the twentieth century.

With her were her two sons: Ronald, now better known to us as J.R.R. Tolkien, and Hilary, his younger brother. Hilary was born in 1894 and in later life became a smallholder in the Evesham area of Worcestershire. They travelled back to England on the Union Line steamer the *Guelph* built in 1894 by Harland and Wolff at Belfast. After leaving Cape Town it called at Tenerife before finally docking at Southampton in England. The family then travelled, most likely, by train to Birmingham New Street station and then by steam tram to King's Heath. It was the brothers' first trip to England to see their grandparents and they were to stay at Mabel's parents' house in Ashfield Road, King's Heath. The three-storey house, built in the late Victorian period, was a short walk from King's Heath railway station and busy High Street, but views of the surrounding countryside could be seen from the top floor.

The memory of the King's Heath area must have been strong in Tolkien's mind as a part of it appears in the chapter 'Three is Company' in *The Fellowship of the Ring*. Frodo, Sam and Pippin are three of the four Hobbits that go on the quest. They are pretending to move house from Bag End to a house in Crickhollow and they pass through Green Hill County. At one end of Ashfield Road, if you turn left, the road runs up a small steep hill, which was locally known as Green Hill, and there is even a Green Hill Road near the top of the hill. They also pass through Woody End on this part of the journey and a few miles south of Birmingham is a small village still called Wood End.

Tolkien describes Hobbits in part of the Prologue to *The Lord of the Rings: For they are a little people, smaller than Dwarves: less stout and stocky, that is, even when they are actually much shorter. Their*

Maitland Street, Bloemfontein in the Orange Free State, Southern Africa, *c.* 1900.

The Union Line steamer *Guelph* on which Mabel Tolkien returned to England with her two sons Ronald and Hilary in 1895.

height is variable, ranging between two and four feet of our measure. They seldom now reach three feet; but they have dwindled, they say, and in ancient days they were taller. (*The Lord of the Rings*, Prologue, Concerning Hobbits and other matters.)

King's Heath at that time was going through a major building boom and little did they know that one day they would be living in a house built in this boom. The area must have been a very busy place with horses and carts moving building materials and coal, an essential for

New Street station, Birmingham, *c.* 1905.

In those days steam trams travelled from the city centre to King's Heath and postcards posted in the morning could be delivered by the evening.

life in the late Victorian period and with steam-powered trams clanking up and down the High Street.

Sadly, in 1896 they received news that Arthur Tolkien had died in Bloemfontein and Mabel decided that she, Ronald and Hilary were going to stay in England.

Above: Ashfield Road photographed from just outside the house of Mabel Tolkien's parents in the early years of the twentieth century.

Right: Tolkien's grandparents' house as it is today.

Opposite:
Top: King's Heath High Street with a tram travelling down it from Moseley Village and the city centre, *c.* 1910.

Middle: King's Heath High Street at the junction of York Road and Heathfield Road.

Bottom: Heathfield Road, a quiet side street off King's Heath High Street, *c.* 1910.

The sign on Greenhill Road, Moseley, today. The Hobbits pass through Green Hill country on the way to Crickhollow.

The village sign for Wood End, just south of Birmingham near Tanworth-in-Arden. Woody End appears in *The Lord of the Rings*.

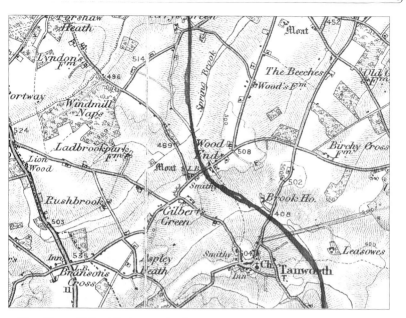

The village of Wood End, 1900. (Ordnance Survey, Worcestershire sheet X1 NW Warwickshire X1X NW)

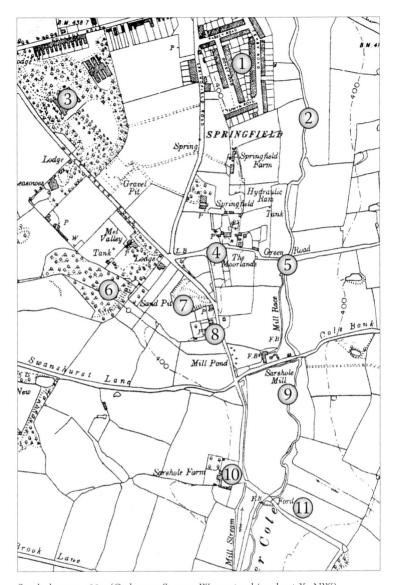

Sarehole area, 1882. (Ordnance Survey, Worcestershire sheet X1 NW)

① Tunnel-back Victorian terraced housing

② River Cole ⑦ Sandpit

③ Moseley School ⑧ 5 Gracewell Cottages

④ The Moorlands and Chalet ⑨ Sarehole Mill

⑤ Ford at Green Lane ⑩ Robin Hood Lane Ford

⑥ Moseley Bog ⑪ Sarehole Farm

Chapter 2

Sarehole

Mabel rented a small house about two miles away from King's Heath in the small rural hamlet of Sarehole in the county of Worcestershire. This small hamlet and surrounding countryside was to become a very important place in Tolkien's later life when writing *The Lord of the Rings*.

The house, at the time known as 5 Gracewell Cottages, today 264 Wake Green Road, was a semi-detached house in a group of three built in 1892. The two-storey houses with a part timber-framed appearance were built for the servants and retainers of a solicitor who lived a short walk away in Green Lane, today known as Green Road (plate 2; p. 52).

This house stood beside a sleepy lane leading into Moseley Village and the city centre; traffic would have been horses and carts and wagons with the odd herd of sheep or cattle being driven into the city market. There would have been no gas or electric lights and no street lighting so at night the family would have used candles or oil lamps. They would have heard and smelt the city if the wind was blowing in the right direction and heard the steam trains coming and going through the day and night.

This was an age when everyone would have had to walk to get their daily needs and to visit friends and relatives and it would have been a good walk to get to the nearest tram line. So 5 Gracewell Cottages would have been quite isolated in a rural setting, but also not too far from the great city of Birmingham at the height of the Victorian period. But at night with the curtains drawn and a fire in the hearth it would have been a cosy place to be.

Just over the road from Gracewell Cottages in the 1890s stood two other cottages. These were replaced in 1910 by what looked like a Tudor manor house with timber framing and brick infill panels. The house, called Millmead, had, as far as one can tell, nothing to do with the Tolkiens, but timber-framed buildings like it would have been a common sight in the area during the family's time at Sarehole,

The little hamlet of Sarehole, *c.* 1908, looking up Wake Green Road towards Moseley Village with Gracewell Cottages, home of the Tolkiens, on the left.

Gracewell Cottages today, now 264 Wake Green Road and part of Gracewell Homes Foster Trust for retired ladies.

although not in such good condition as this one was. It has a row of trees in front of it that are taking on Ent-like appearance as the years go by. Merry and Pippin encounter an Ent called Treebeard in the Forest of Fangorn when escaping from the soldiers – called Orcs – of the Dark Lord. Their description gives a clear vision of an Ent: *They found that they were looking at a most extraordinary face. It belonged to a large Man-like, almost Troll–like, figure, at least fourteen foot high, very sturdy, with a tall head, and hardly any neck... The large feet had seven toes each. The lower part of the long face was covered with a sweeping grey beard, bushy, almost twiggy at the roots, thin and mossy at the ends* (*The Two Towers*, Treebeard.) (plate 1; p. 49)

Treebeard, who plays a major part in *The Lord of the Rings*, describes Ents: *We are tree-herds, we old Ents. Few enough of us are left now. Sheep get like shepherd, and shepherds like sheep, it is said; but slowly, and neither have long in the world. It is quicker and closer with trees and Ents* (*The Two Towers*, Treebeard.)

A short walk up the hill towards Moseley Village and you will come to an iron fence through which you will see a wooded area, known locally as The Dell. But this is not the '…wonderful dell with flowers' that Ronald talked about, but a sandpit, and what a great place for Ronald and Hilary to play in during their time at Gracewell Cottages. (plates 3, 4; pp 52-3)

This sandpit must be the model for the sand and gravel pits in *The Return of the King*. When the Hobbits return to the Shire they find the house of Sam's father, The Gaffer, at Bagshot Row has been pulled down to make way for a sand and gravel pit. *Bagshot Row was a yawning sand and gravel quarry* (*The Return of the King*, The Scouring of the Shire.) *One of the first things done in Hobbiton, before even the removal of the new mill, was the clearing of the Hill and Bag End, and the restoration of Bagshot Row. The front of the new sand-pit was all levelled and made into a large sheltered garden, and new holes dug in the southward face, back into the Hill, and were lined with brick* (*The Return of the King*, The Grey Havens.)

Well this sandpit has not been filled in or levelled, but has become a wooded wildlife garden. Also a sandpit is the place where the Ruffians are buried after the Battle of Bywater: *At last all was over. Nearly seventy of the ruffians lay dead on the field, and a dozen were prisoners. Nineteen Hobbits were killed, and some thirty were wounded. The dead ruffians were laden on wagons and hauled off to an old sand-pit nearby and buried: in the Battle Pit, as it was afterwards called* (*The Return of the King*, The Scouring of the Shire.) This burial has echoes of the mass graves witnessed by Tolkien and used for dead soldiers after the battles on the Western Front in the First World War.

Just a little way up Wake Green Road stood the impressive Pine Dell Hydropathic Establishment and Moseley Botanical Gardens.

Millmead House, with some Ent-like trees guarding its garden.

Wake Green Road seen here a few years after the Tolkiens had moved away from Gracewell Cottages The sandpit lay just behind the hedge on the right-hand side. The cottage in the foreground is where a Mrs Hunt lived.

Built in the 1850s in the Gothic style with gargoyles that look very Orc-like, it was first called Spring Hill College and served as a non-conformist training college, opened in 1857. In 1886 this college then relocated to Oxford as Mansfield College. The building became Pine Dell Hydropathic Establishment and Moseley Botanical Gardens in 1892, but only lasted in this form till 1900.

Back in 1897 a garden party was held there to celebrate Queen Victoria's jubilee, which the family is believed to have gone to. As part

Above: Pine Dell Hydropathic Establishment and Moseley Botanical Gardens, formally Spring Hill College. (courtesy of Terry Carter)

Right: Spring Hill College after building renovations.

of the celebrations they had electric illuminations and fireworks. This does have echoes at the very beginning of *The Lord of the Rings* in 'A Long-expected Party' when Gandalf brings the fireworks for Bilbo's and Frodo's birthday party. A jubilee party planned months before would appear to a small boy as 'a long-expected party'. *The fireworks were by Gandalf: they were not only brought by him, but designed and made by him; and the special effects, set pieces, and flights of rockets were let off by him. But there was also a generous distribution of squibs,*

Some of these great old beech trees have faces appearing out of their trunks.

crackers, backarappers, sparklers, torches, dwarf-candles, elf-foun-
tains, goblin-barkers and thunderclaps. They were all superb. The art
of Gandalf improved with age. (*The Fellowship of the Ring*, A Long-
expected Party.)

In a strange twist of fate Hilary Tolkien found himself back there in
1915 as a member of the drums and bugles section of the 3ʳᵈ Birmingham
Battalion. The building had been commandeered by the military. His
main job in the battalion on active service was as a stretcher-bearer.
Did he remember his childhood visit some eighteen years before?

Today this building is part of a modern comprehensive school and
sixth form college. Following a major renovation in the late 1990s
the name Spring Hill College has been restored to the building, now
largely used by the sixth form college. It looks magical when illuminated at night. (plate 5; p. 56)

'The wonderful dell with flowers' lay a short walk across the fields
behind Gracewell Cottages. The fields had names like Old Pool
Meadow and Hilly Field and were divided up by the old head-race
for Greet Mill Pool and the brook was called Coldbath Brook as it is
today. These fields have now disappeared under a modern housing
estate. Greet Mill Pool had been, up to the 1850s, one of the storage
pools for Sarehole Mill, but was drained around this time and had
become wooded and most likely full of spring flowers. Today this is
called Moseley Bog and is a local nature reserve and part of The Shire
Country Park. (plate 6; p. 56)

Back then, in a time before the use of modern herbicides, an open,
barren piece of ground would rapidly be taken over by flowers, ferns,
blackberries and trees. The boys, having crossed the fields, would scram-
ble over the old earthen dam into this magical world of light and shade
and trees with the Coldbath Brook babbling through it. Everything is
much larger when recalled by a child. (plate 7; p. 57)

Tolkien's childhood memory of this place must have fired his imagination when writing about 'The Old Forest and Fangorn' in *The Lord of*
the Rings: *But the Forest is queer. Everything in it is very much more alive,*
more aware of what is going on, so to speak, than things are in the Shire.
And the trees do not like strangers. They watch you. They are usually
content merely to watch you, as long as daylight lasts, and don't do much.
(*The Fellowship of the Ring*, The Old Forest.) (plate 8; p. 60)

Many springs flow into this wooded dell and areas of marsh and
pools of water can still be seen today and in the late summer there
are plenty of midges to bite you. (plates 9, 10; pp. 61, 64) While the
Hobbits are crossing Midgewater Marshes, Pippin and Sam have this
conversation: *'I am being eaten alive!' cried Pippin. 'Midgewater! There*
are more midges than water!' 'What do they live on when they can't get
hobbit?' asked Sam, scratching his neck. (*The Fellowship of the Ring*, A
Knife in the Dark.) (plates 11 12; pp. 64, 65)

There are a number of marshes in *The Lord of the Rings*. But to find the Dead Marshes we would have to travel to the Western Front in 1916 and the Battle of the Somme, with shell holes full of water and bodies in the water. While crossing the Dead Marshes Sam and Frodo ask Gollum about them and Gollum explains: *All dead, all rotten. Elves and Men and Orcs. The Dead Marshes. There was a great battle long ago, yes, so they told him when Sméagol was young, when I was young before the Precious came. It was a great battle. Tall Men with long swords, and terrible Elves, and Orcses shrieking. They fought on the plain for days and months at the Black Gates. But the Marshes have grown since then, swallowed up the graves; always creeping, creeping.* (*The Two Towers*, The Passage of the Marshes.)

A scene on the Western Front during the First World War. Shell holes full of water that could be a vision of the Dead Marshes.

A vision of hell from the Western Front, with shell holes as far as the eye can see.

The journey across the fields to get to this magical place was not without its perils, as Hilary Tolkien recalled in later life, because the farmer who worked the land was not very pleased by trespassers. Once he chased Ronald for picking mushrooms on his land. The boys nicknamed him the 'Black Ogre' and he lived at Sarehole Farm a short distance from Sarehole Mill. Is Ronald getting his revenge in *The Lord of the Rings* with Farmer Maggot and the mushrooms incident of Frodo's youth recalled on the journey to Crickhollow when they met Farmer Maggot? Frodo is explaining to Sam and Pippin about Farmer Maggot as they reach his land on the way to Crickhollow: *'but all the same,' he added with a shame-faced laugh, 'I am terrified of him and his dogs. I have avoided his farm for years and years. He caught me several times trespassing after mushrooms, when I was a youngster at Brandy Hall. On the last occasion he beat me, and took me and showed me to his dogs. "See, lads," he said, "next time this young varmint sets foot on my land, you can eat him.' (The Fellowship of the Ring,* A Shortcut to Mushrooms.)

A short walk from Gracewell Cottages brought you to Green Lane – today called Green Road – and further down the lane in the 1890s there was a grand mansion called Spartans, built in the late Georgian period and demolished after the Second World War, and a Victorian farm called Moorlands.

A little further down the lane stands a timber-framed farmhouse from the Stuart period with a barn behind it. The front of the farmhouse is plastered over as it was in the 1890s and it is locally known as the Chalet. Some fine groups of houseleeks can be seen growing on the roof of the Chalet and these are believed in folklore to stop the house from being struck by lightning.

At the bottom of the hill one reaches the ford across the River Cole: one of the few still open to road traffic in Birmingham. The ford may have played a role years later in *The Lord of the Rings* because this one is prone to flash floods. Even today unwary car drivers can be washed down the river during a flood. This would make it a good model for the ford at Bruinen where the Black Riders are washed away whilst chasing the wounded Frodo on his way to Rivendell: *...a noise of loud waters rolling many stones. Dimly Frodo saw the river below him rise, and down along its course there came a plumed cavalry of waves. White flames seemed to Frodo to flicker on their crests and he half fancied that he saw amid the water white riders upon white horses with frothing manes. The three Riders that were still in the midst of the ford were overwhelmed: they disappeared, buried suddenly under angry foam.* (*The Fellowship of the Ring,* Flight to the Ford.) (plate 13; p. 65)

The wound given to Frodo by the Black Rider recalls shrapnel wounds suffered by solders in the First World War caused by shell splinters piercing their bodies.

The Moorlands as it is today (2006).

The Chalet in Green Lane as it is today (2006).

The ivy-covered Chalet and lane leading down to the ford, *c.* 1910.

The ford across the River Cole at Green Lane, now called Green Road, early twentieth century.

Sarehole Mill in around 1890. George Andrew was the miller at the time and he is seen here at work with his son, called the 'White Ogre' by the Tolkien brothers. (courtesy of Birmingham Library Services)

Chapter 3

Sarehole Mill

Every time the Tolkiens walked out of the front door of 5 Gracewell Cottages, the thing that would have dominated the view was Sarehole Mill and its millpond just across the meadow from the cottage. Today trees block the view. Back in those days Sarehole was spelt as two words: Sare Hole and the 'hole' part of the word most likely comes from 'holm' which means flood meadow. (plate 14; p. 68)

In the Foreword to *The Lord of the Rings* the miller and his son are mentioned; the miller in Tolkien's day was George Andrew. *Recently I saw in a paper a picture of the decrepitude of the once thriving corn-mill beside its pool that long ago seemed to me so important. I never liked the looks of the Young miller, but his father, the Old miller, had a black beard, and he was not named Sandyman* (*The Lord of the Rings*, Foreword.)

Sarehole Mill and its surrounding infrastructure were destined to play a major role in the development of the world of Middle-earth in later years. The mill must have been a marvel and wonder to the two brothers, with its two massive waterwheels, gears, steam engine and massive chimney and was just over the road from their home. (plates 15, 16, 17; pp 68, 69) There would have been carts coming and going and even carts in the fords at Green Lane or Robin Hood Lane just a little way from the mill, soaking the wood in their wheels to make it swell firmly back into the iron rim and make the cart last a few more trips before having to replace the wheels.

The miller, George Andrew senior, operated Sarehole Mill at that time when many of the inland watermills of England had fallen on hard times. This was because they were unable to compete with the large modern mills at the ports grinding imported grain and producing white flour. To make a living they ground animal bones for fertiliser and ground animal feed for local farms. This produced much dust and the miller would come out of the mill to chase off the Tolkien boys, for their own safety, covered in dust and surrounded in clouds of dust. They nicknamed his son George Andrew junior the 'White Ogre'.

Sarehole Mill as it would have been seen by the Tolkien brothers as they emerged from their front door. When this picture postcard was made at the turn of the twentieth century the name was written as Sare Hole.

The mill and mill yard today.

Millers were not always popular people in rural England in the past. Millers sometimes took around 6% of the flour they produced as payment. This led to disputes between the miller and the customer, because it was often alleged that the miller was taking more than he was entitled to. But by the late Victorian period payment was usually in cash for grinding work at the mill. Sandyman the miller in Hobbiton is not a very pleasant character in *The Lord of the Rings*.

The mill, with its smoking chimney, makes several appearances in *The Lord of the Rings*. When Sam is looking into the Lady Galadriel's mirror he sees the mill of Hobbiton with a smoking chimney discharging pollution into the environment: *But now Sam noticed that the Old Mill had vanished, and a large red-brick building was put up where it had stood. Lots of folk were busily at work. There was a tall red chimney nearby. Black smoke seemed to cloud the surface of the Mirror.* (*The Fellowship of the Ring*, The Mirror of Galadriel.) This is a vision of the mill as it was in *The Return of the King* when the Hobbits return to the Shire and find that it has become the mill in vision. *Take Sandyman's mill now. Pimple knocked it down almost as soon as he came to Bag End. Then he brought in a lot o' dirty-looking Men to build a bigger one and fill it full o' wheels and outlandish contraptions.* (*The Return of the King*, The Scouring of the Shire.) So the mill we see today at Sarehole with its three-storey brick building and chimney is Ted Sandyman's mill in *The Lord of the Rings.*

The mill closed in 1919 and the miller's son lived on till 1959 and operated as a florist with greenhouses around the mill. The solicitor from Green Lane, A.H. Foster, purchased the mill and surrounding meadows to stop them being built on. He bequeathed it to the City of Birmingham after the miller's son had passed away. Foster himself died in November 1929 and left the then huge sum of £145,000 to set up the Gracewell Homes Foster Trust for spinster or widowed ladies and the Gracewell Cottages became the first building used. After the First World War the demand for homes for widows was high and since those days it has expanded further, now housing up to sixty-one women, widowed or unmarried.

By the 1960s the mill was in very poor shape and a very creepy place at night from my young imagination: I used to change buses there on my way home and standing alone there at the bus stop was not a pleasant experience. (I think I had also just read at that time *Something Wicked This Way Comes* by Ray Bradbury!) The mill was saved by a local public campaign and subscription. One of the people who donated money was none other than J.R.R. Tolkien himself and the mill later opened as a working museum in 1969. On the last Sunday of each month from April to October it grinds corn and the whole building rocks and rolls, but sadly the flour cannot be used nowadays because the mill has non-approved wooden chutes and hoppers.

One of the many willow trees growing around the millpond today.

At the time the family lived at Gracewell Cottages there grew a large willow tree beside the millpond, which for some unknown reason was cut down by a local butcher. The boys used to climb this tree and they were upset by its pointless destruction as it was then left to rot. But its descendants are now slowly choking the far end of the mill pool. (plate 18; p. 72)

Strangely Old Man Willow in *The Lord of the Rings* is a rather evil character too. *'What?' shouts Tom Bombadil, leaping up in the air. 'Old Man Willow? Naught worse than that, eh? That can soon be mended. I know the tune for him. Old grey Willow-man! I'll freeze his marrow cold, if he don't behave himself. I'll sing his roots off. I'll sing a wind up and blow leaf and branch away. Old Man Willow!'* (*The Fellowship of the Ring*, The Old Forest.)

A modern view of the mill chimney. It belched black smoke when the steam engine was operating.

A blue plaque at Sarehole Mill records the associations of Matthew Boulton, the engineer, and J.R.R. Tolkien with Sarehole Mill – strange bedfellows indeed!

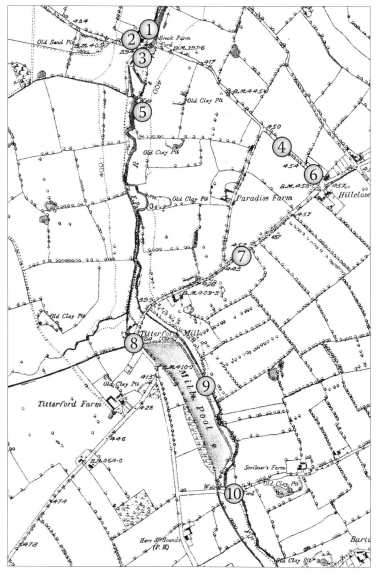

The Dingles and Titterford area, 1882. (Ordnance Survey, Worcestershire sheet X1 NW)

1. Brook Farm
2. Little Sarehole Farm
3. Webb Lane and Brook Lane Ford
4. Webb Lane
5. Whyrl Hole and Weir
6. Sparks Brothers Smithy
7. Highfield Road
8. Titterford Mill
9. River Cole
10. Scriber's Lane Ford

Chapter 4

The Cole Valley

The Cole Valley is now part of The Shire Country Park created in 2005 and named in recognition of Tolkien's association with the area. Tolkien took the idea of the Hobbits from the village people and children in the area of Sarehole and the Cole Valley. He lived in this area during his formative years and it was the inspiration for the Shire, the area where the Hobbits live in *The Hobbit* and *The Lord of the Rings.*

This chapter will be like travelling through the Cole Valley section of The Shire Country Park, but in the late Victorian and Edwardian period. As will be seen, much remains that the Tolkien brothers would have been familiar with.

Just below Sarehole Mill flows the River Cole and the fords on the river hold special significance in the world of Middle-earth. The first ford going up the river in the 1890s was where Wake Green Road and Robin Hood Lane crossed the river and it provided a good opportunity for animals being driven to market in Birmingham to be watered. (plate 19; p. 72)

Today the ford is hard to find, but is still marked by thick wooden posts. This is because in 1906 a new railway line marched across the landscape and Robin Hood Lane and Webb Lane were moved to their present locations.

Tolkien might have witnessed the building of this railway line, and the building of railways is mentioned in the Foreword of *The Lord of the Rings*: *The country in which I lived in childhood was being shabbily destroyed before I was ten, in the days when motor-cars were rare objects (I had never seen one) and men were still building suburban railways.* (*The Lord of the Rings*, Foreword.)

I think that it is likely that the character of Tom Bombadil is based on the Green Man, the spirit of the wild wood in English folklore. Other names for the Green Man are Jack in the Green and Robin Hood. *'Fair lady!' said Frodo again after a while. 'Tell me, if my asking does not seem foolish, who is Tom Bombadil?' 'He is,' said Goldberry,*

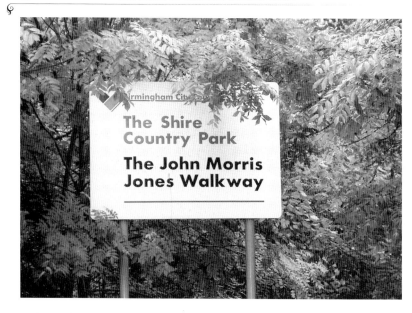

The newly created Shire Country Park, so-named because of Tolkien's connections with the area. John Morris Jones was a local historian and teacher who wrote about the Cole Valley and other parts of Birmingham.

The last days of the ford at the junction of Robin Hood Lane and Wake Green Road in Sarehole, 1906. The new railway embankment can be seen on the horizon.

Robin Hood Lane a little way up from the ford through the River Cole, *c.* 1910.

staying her swift movement and smiling. Frodo looked at her question-ingly. 'He is, as you have seen him,' she said in answer to his look. 'He is the Master of wood, water and hill.' (The Fellowship of the Ring, In the House of Tom Bombadil.)

During the late nineteenth and early twentieth centuries there was a great revival of the Green Men in decorations on buildings, often made in terracotta, and today there are around 100 to be found in Birmingham city centre alone. (plate 20; p. 73)

Just a short walk from the ford stood Sarehole Farm, now sadly demol-ished, but at that time home to a farmer called Charles William Purser. In 1933 Tolkien returned to Birmingham with his family to visit relations and recorded the following in his diary: *The old mill still stands, and Mrs Hunt's still sticks out into the road as it turns uphill; but the crossing beyond the now fenced-in pool, where the bluebell lane ran down into the mill lane, is now a dangerous crossing alive with motors and red lights. The White Ogre's house (which the children were excited to see) is become a petrol station. (J.R.R Tolkien: A Biography* by Humphrey Carpenter.)

Personal research has shown that the 'White Ogre', George Andrew junior, lived all his life at Sarehole Mill. The building that had become a petrol station was Sarehole Farm and home also to the 'Black Ogre'. Mrs Hunt's house can clearly be seen sticking out into the road on a contemporary photograph (p. 26) but it has also been demolished since then.

Moving along the River Cole one enters an area locally known as the Dingles. This charming piece of river valley, with tree-lined banks and open meadows, is still a treasure today, even though twentieth-century houses now hem it in. In the spring many parts of this valley give off the heady smell of the wild garlic that grows in the damper

Sarehole Farm, home of the 'Black Ogre'. (courtesy of Birmingham Library Services)

parts. The hay meadows are cut in the late summer to encourage the growth of wild flowers. On a summer's day it is just possible to imagine one is back in the 1890s in a landscape that has not changed much except that all of the farms have gone.

As we move up the valley, the next ford on the River Cole is where Brook Lane and the then Webb Lane used to cross the river. Well, there are a few large spiders in Middle-earth. Today the ford has gone with the building of the railway, but the brick-built Four Arches Bridge is still to be seen. (plates 21, 22; pp. 72, 76)

In the 1890s there was a group of farm buildings at the ford side: these were Brook and Little Sarehole farms. Also, and still visible today, is an overflow from Sarehole Mill head-race that allowed water to be discharged back into the river at times of flood. (plate 23; p. 76)

Back in the 1890s, before the coming of the railway, one could walk up Webb Lane, but today you would have to go back to Robin Hood Lane and under the railway bridge to reach it. Even today the lane still has a rural feel to it with most of the old hedges still evident. (plate 24; p. 77)

At the end of the lane in those times stood a blacksmith's shop and cart and wagon workshop, run by the Sparks brothers. (What a great name for blacksmiths!) Carts were an everyday sight in those days just as are lorries and vans today.

A common sight of Tolkien's youth would have been blacksmiths' forges. There would have been many in a world powered mainly by

The River Cole meandering through the Dingles.

Two young lads in The Dingles around 1907.

horses and just so that you could not mistake them for anything else, many forges had doors made in the shape of a horseshoe. Could a long-held memory of these have led Tolkien to write about Hobbits having round doors to their homes? *In a hole in the ground lived a hobbit. Not a nasty, dirty, wet hole, filled with the ends of worms and an oozy smell, nor yet a dry, bare, sandy hole with nothing in it to sit down on or to eat: it was a hobbit-hole, and that means comfort. It had a*

Part of the head-race taking water through The Dingles to Sarehole Mill.

Four Arches Bridge across the River Cole and up Webb Lane, *c.* 1910.

perfectly round door like a porthole, painted green, with a shiny yellow brass knob in the exact middle. (*The Hobbit,* An Unexpected Party.)

Returning to the Cole Valley a little further up the river, we come to a small bridge. This place is called Whyrl-hole and here the water would swirl in a pool in the river. This is the point where the head-race for Sarehole Mill starts and back in 1768 a group of workmen with picks, shovels and wheelbarrows dug this channel. The head-race is just under 4 metres wide and around 2,400 metres in length and some

Down Webb Lane to the ford, Brook Farm and Little Sarehole Farm.

of it is still there today, but a century ago it would have been a very busy water channel.

Still today in some of the meadows in the Dingles can be seen the echo of the ridge and furrow method of farming and this could be evidence of mans' farming in the area back to the medieval period.

Further up the River Cole valley one reaches the site of the second mill that Tolkien talks about in the 1966 interview. This, back then, was called Titterford Mill. The mill was built in 1779 but the river crossing below it is an ancient place mentioned back in 1546. The mill was damaged by fire in the 1920s and demolished and the name was changed in the 1920s to Trittiford Mill Pool when the modern housing was built. This name change was most likely made for reasons of good taste at the time, but it is a shame because Titterford probably has a Scandinavian language origin meaning either small ford or the ford where small birds are found.

The mill pool is very long and thin and may be the model for the Long Lake in *The Hobbit*. Today the mill pool is a haven for wildlife, including, and a little strange for a suburb of Birmingham, seagulls. Canada geese and mink also live here today. (plate 25; p. 77). At the end of the millpond the head-race and overflow weir can still be seen and a little way down Scribers Lane another ford crosses the River Cole, today closed to motor traffic.

The Tolkien brothers would also have been familiar with a sight a little further up the Cole Valley of an old tower windmill, blown up in 1957, which stood on a small hill beside Brampton's Pool, a pool made as a fish-pond and not a millpond.

The Sparks brothers' smithy and cart and wagon workshops at the end of Webb Lane, Hall Green.

Enamelled plate from a cart or wagon made by the Sparks brothers.

The brothers may also have carried on further up the valley, passing another Green Lane with a ford across the River Cole, to the aqueduct carrying the Stratford on Avon Canal over the river and Aqueduct Lane. But it would have been a long walk back to Sarehole, especially if you only had Hobbit-sized legs.

1 *Above:* One of the many Ent-like trees in the area. *Left:* Ent-like tree outside Mill Mead House.

The forge at Claverdon near Henley-in-Arden, *c.* 1910. Horseshoe-shaped doors were a common sight on blacksmiths' forges in Tolkien's time.

Today a firm selling wood-burning stoves uses the forge at Claverdon.

After four years at Sarehole, Mabel, Ronald and Hilary moved up the Wake Green Road to the village of Moseley. They most likely would have moved their household goods by horse and cart the mile and a half distance.

A heavily loaded hay cart of Tolkien's Birmingham period.

Titterford Mill Pool in the early twentieth century. The name was later changed to Trittiford.

2 Gracewell Cottages through the trees from the field beside Sarehole Mill.

3 The sandpit floor is now crowded with trees and spring flowering plants and is an example of how nature repairs the destruction of man.

4 The rim of the sandpit with an Ent-like tree clinging on for dear life.

Titterford Mill, Yardley Wood, *c.* 1900. The mill is sadly now lost.

Canada geese on Trittiford Mill Pool in late spring.

Opposite:
Colebrook Priory area, 1882. (Ordnance Survey, Worcestershire Sheet X1 SW, Warwickshire sheet X1X SW)

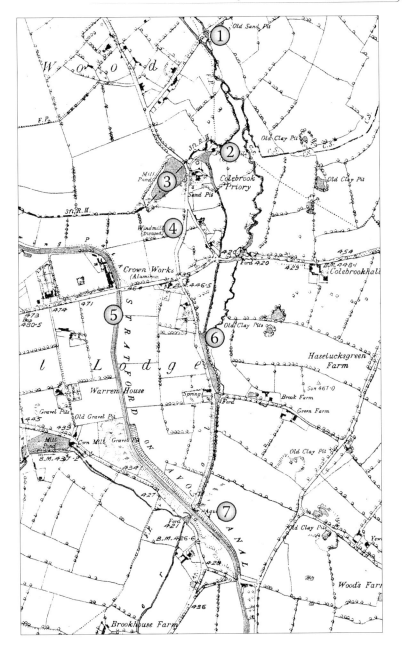

1) Slade Lane and Baldwin Lane Ford   5) Canal

2) Priory Mill   6) River Cole

3) Bampton's Pool   7) Aqueduct

4) Tower Windmill

5 Spring Hill College as it looks after its renovation.

6 Moseley Bog, a wonderful dell of flowers at springtime.

7 The sleeper walkway in Moseley Bog along the top of the old dam that held the water back to create Greet Mill Pool.

The ford at Scriber's Lane at the end of Titterford Pool, *c.* 1905.

The ford at Scribers Lane today looking unchanged but for graffiti on the bridge, most likely done by modern-day Orcs.

The old tower windmill at Brampton's Pool, Yardley Wood.

The now sadly lost windmill that stood above Brampton's Pool.

8 Giant beech trees that still stand beside the fields (playing fields today) just above Moseley Bog.

9 A marshy part of Moseley Bog.

Brampton's Pool today is home to a variety of waterfowl.

The ford where another Green Lane crosses the River Cole to join Aqueduct Lane, Yardley Wood, *c.* 1905.

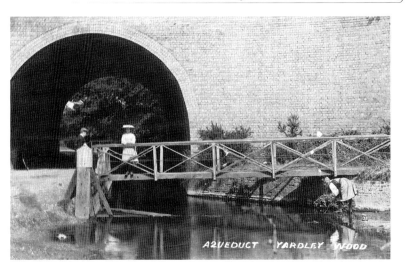

The aqueduct carries the Birmingham to Stratford Canal over the River Cole and Aqueduct Lane. This view, from around 1905, is hardly changed today, except perhaps for the style of dress of people looking at the water.

Wake Green Road just before entering Moseley village, *c.* 1905.

10 *Left:* Wood Anemones flowering in the spring in Moseley Bog.

11 *Below:* One of the Ent-like trees at the top of Moseley Bog with the path covered with leaves.

12 *Right:* Another Ent-like tree in Moseley Bog, about to walk away?

13 A Black Rider approaching the ford at Green Road at the Tolkien Weekend 2002. The rider was Mark Vance and the horse was Equinox, who refused to cross the ford; maybe she had read the book.

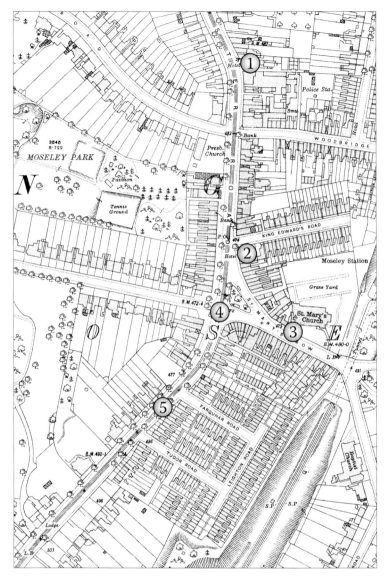

Moseley Village, 1913. (courtesy Alan Godfrey Maps)

1. Prince of Wales public house
2. Fighting Cocks public house
3. St Mary's Row
4. Tram Lines
5. Moseley Road

Chapter 5

Moseley Village

he move to Moseley Village would have brought a major change in the family's life: the quiet rural hamlet of Sarehole and the busy Victorian suburb of Moseley were like chalk and cheese. *His mother had rented a small house on the main road in the suburb of Moseley, and the view from the windows was a sad contrast to the Warwickshire countryside: trams struggling up the hill, the drab faces of passers-by, and in the distance the smoking factory chimneys of Sparkbrook and Small Heath. (*J.R.R Tolkien*: A Biography* by Humphrey Carpenter.)

The steam trams may have been a help to Mabel Tolkien who was living on a limited income, having been a widow now for four years. The trams may have been a blight on the housing on the route. A postcard published to commemorate the end of the tram service in 1906 said: 'Made the houses all "To Let" along the line'. So the rents would probably have been lower than those in quieter streets away from the line. This road also runs directly into Birmingham city centre and was very busy with all kinds of traffic including, by this time, the odd motorcar too. But the major noise and disturbance to life in this location was caused by the steam-driven trams that ploughed up and down the hill, taking people to and from the city centre. There was even a protest movement against their use in Moseley. They would have had to get up a good head of steam to climb the hill into King's Heath. Yet these noisy machines were the very reason that the family moved here because Ronald was now at school in the city centre at King Edward VI School and needed to live on a more convenient route to get there. This school building was demolished some years after Ronald left, and the school moved out to Edgbaston, but is still remembered on the site on New Street by a stylish 1930s building called King Edward House.

14 Modern view of the mill and millpond on a summer's day.

15 Part of the gear train used to transfer power from the waterwheel to the grinding stone.

16 Water pouring onto the waterwheel to power the mill.

17 The steam engine used to drive the mill when water levels were too low to turn the wheels.

Right: Moseley Road today with some of those stylish towers recognisable in the earlier view still present.

Below: A steam tram on the Moseley Road.

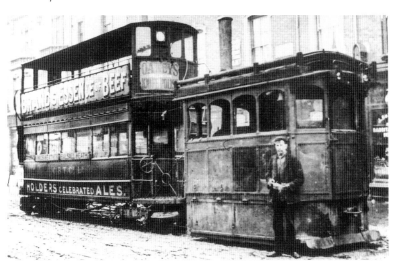

Opposite

Top: Moseley Village High Street looking towards King's Heath, *c.* 1905. The house rented by Mabel Tolkien was just round the corner to the right. The Fighting Cocks public house is on the left-hand side of the picture.

Middle: St Mary's Row in Moseley Village, *c.* 1905.

Bottom: Moseley Road, looking towards Birmingham, *c.* 1910.

18 Willows and reeds are taking over the end of the millpond.

19 The old Robin Hood Lane as it is today.

20 Three terra-cotta Green Men forming part of the decoration above the entrance to the Midland Hotel, erected in 1902, just around the corner from King Edward VI School which Tolkien attended.

21 The Four Arches Bridge on a spring morning, surrounded with spring flowers.

A Souvenir to be kept

In Loving Memory

OF THE

Old Steam Trams,

which succumbed to an
Electric Shock.   Dec. 31st, 1906.

1.

Though your breath it smelt like sulphur
And your sides were bare of paint
And you could'nt be called an ornament to the Street!
And oft our cash we've had to look for
Whilst some 14 stone conductor
Got the fares on top while standing on our feet!

2.

Though the rattle and the roar
As upon your way you "tore"
Made the houses all to LET along the line!
Though your rocking made us bilious
And your lurching made us faint
And we thought that you would bust up any time!

3.

Still you had your points old Lumberer
For you took us all the way.
We shall miss you, though we've hissed you it is true
Though rude boys oft called you "rotten"
You are gone, but not forgotten
Nevermore we'll gaze upon you but—
            We'll never forget you.

P.S.

Do you ask me, O Departed!
How it was that though we smarted
And we grumbled—still we used you every day?
Don't crow, Steam Tram—you've no cause to,
Recollect that we were forced to,
Ride on you or WALK, O Lost One
For you were.................THE ONLY WAY.

SCOTT RUSSELL & CO., B'HAM. No. 129.   F.S.R.

Top: A postcard that celebrated the steam trams going out of service at the end of 1906. They were replaced by electrically powered trams.

Middle: King Edward VI Grammar School, Birmingham, as it would have looked in Tolkien's time.

Left: A blue plaque on King Edward House recording a school's presence on this site for almost 400 years.

King Edward Chapel was moved from the centre of Birmingham to its present site in Edgbaston. Inside are recorded names of old boys who died in the armed services. A number of Tolkien's school friends from before the First World War are recorded there.

A view up Corporation Street that would have been familiar to Tolkien and his school friends as they walked to Barrow's Stores from school to take tea. The store survived until the 1960s but the site has now been redeveloped.

22 The view from the Four Arches Bridge up the River Cole in the spring.

23 Wild garlic growing in the head-race that used to take the water to Sarehole Mill just up from the Four Arches Bridge.

24 Webb Lane as it
looks today

25 Trittiford Pool on a summer's day.

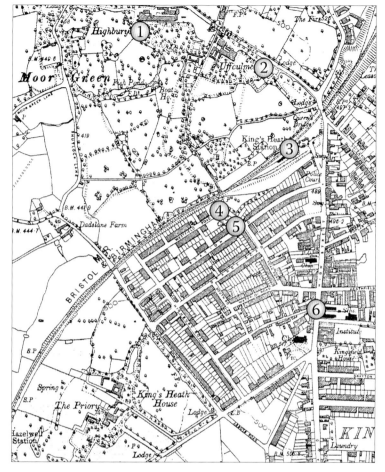

King's Heath area, 1882. (Ordnance Survey, Worcestershire sheet X1 NW, Warwickshire X1X NW)

1. Highbury
2. Uffculmbe
3. King's Heath Railway Station
4. Westfield Road
5. St Dunstan's RC Church
6. King's Heath High Street

Chapter 6

Return to King's Heath

After a short period in Moseley the Tolkiens moved back to King's Heath. The new address was Westfield Road on the Grange Estate, which was still being built and would have still been busy with carts of bricks, timber and tiles and workmen when they arrived.

The reason for the move was that Mabel had become a Roman Catholic and the attraction was a small Catholic church, St Dunstan's, that had opened in Westfield Road in December 1896 (now moved to the other side of the High Street). The church building was made of iron sheets with the inside clad with pine boards. Their house in Westfield Road was of a common design for the period, being a three-bedroom tunnel-back terraced house. At the bottom of the small garden many new and different worlds could be seen. The Birmingham to Gloucester railway line ran in a shallow cutting right at the end of the garden and a little way up the line was King's Heath railway station with a small marshalling yard. The station is now closed and demolished. Back in the early part of the twentieth century, coal was king and to feed the needs of King's Heath, a huge amount of coal was transported by train to this station, where many local coal merchants had coal storage yards and some even had their own coaltrucks.

Some of the coal trucks in the small marshalling yard were coming from much further away, including the South Wales coalfield, and it is said that the names on the trucks led to Ronald discovering the Welsh language. *Yet the railway cutting had grass slopes, and here he discovered flowers and plants. And something else attracted his attention: the curious names on the coal–trucks in the siding below, odd names which he did not know how to pronounce but which had a strange appeal to him. So it came about that by pondering over Nantylo, Senghenydd, Blaen - Rhondda, Penrhiwceiber, and Tredegar, he discovered the existence of the Welsh language.* (*J.R.R Tolkien: A Biography* by Humphrey Carpenter.)

Having a busy railway line at the bottom of the garden would have been a wonder to the two young Tolkien brothers. But what lay beyond

26 Highbury today with the ivy and its greenhouse range long gone.

27 Highbury on a moonlit night from an old picture postcard with electric light flooding from the windows.

28 The Spirit of the Woods at the Lickey Hills by Birmingham artist Graham Jones.

A modern view of the terraced house in Westfield Road that was home to the Tolkiens for a short time.

The pine-boarded interior of St Dunstan's church, King's Heath. (courtesy of St Dunstan's church)

King's Heath railway station, *c.* 1910. The station no longer exists.

the railway line was also a wonder for the boys' eyes, because, beyond the farmland, there were mansions, including a very impressive one belonging to Joseph Chamberlain, the Birmingham politician. This house was called Highbury and had been built in a Venetian Gothic style around 1880. Beside the house was a huge range of glasshouses that would have sparkled and glittered in the sunlight. (plate 26; p. 80)

The other mansion, Uffculme, was the home of Richard Cadbury, one of the Cadbury brothers who manufactured chocolate in Bournville a couple of miles away. This house had a huge domed conservatory at the back of the house that is still there today.

At night, Highbury at least, but most likely Uffculme as well, would have been visible, shining and twinkling like Elf palaces. *A gleam of firelight came from the open doors, and soft lights were glowing in many windows.* (*The Fellowship of the Ring*, The Ring Goes South.) (plate 27; p. 80)

Highbury was one of the first houses in Birmingham to be lit by electric light. Electric light to most people in those days would have been a wonder as candles, oil lamps or gaslights would light most homes. Many of the houses that backed onto the railway line had higher rents because of the view of these two grand houses.

The prominent Birmingham architect John H. Chamberlain, not related to Joseph Chamberlain, designed Highbury. Both mansions were used as hospitals in the First World War and still stand today, although Highbury has lost its glasshouses. It is hard to see both buildings today from Westfield Road, as the farmland is now Highbury Park and many trees have been planted that have now grown into large specimens over the years.

29 So-called Perrott's Folly – but not a folly when it was built.

30 A modern view of Edgbaston Reservoir.

31 The clock tower at night, the clock's faces shining like eyes.

After a very short period at this address Mabel, Ronald and Hilary were on the move again, this time back into Birmingham and to the district of Edgbaston, a short distance from the city centre.

A King's Heath coal merchant's wagon. (The Phil Coutanche Collection)

Coal wagon showing the colliery name.

Instructions on the side of a coal truck giving instruction where it is to be returned to when empty.

Highbury, home of Joseph Chamberlain MP, in all its glory, *c.* 1900.

32 *Above:* The top of the Chamberlain Tower – it looks like a good place to imprison a wizard.

33 *Left:* The clock tower leaping skyward.

34 A modern view of the Two Towers with Perrott's Folly in the foreground and the chimney of Edgbaston Water Works in the background.

Part of the huge range of greenhouses at Highbury with the Orchid House in the foreground.

The tropical world inside a conservatory at Highbury.

Uffculme with its huge domed conservatory.

The very grand front entrance to Uffculme.

35 Bag End viewed from the lane.

36 The Malvern Hills looking very misty.

37 St Nicholas' church tower.

Edgbaston area, 1888. (Ordnance Survey, Warwickshire sheet X111 NE)

1. Duchess Road
2. Highfield Road
3. Plough and Harrow
4. The Oratory
5. Oliver Road
6. Perrott's Folly
7. The Ivy Bush public house
8. Edgbaston Waterworks
9. Stirling Road
10. The edge of Edgbaston Reservoir

Chapter 7

Edgbaston and Rednal

The next move was to Oliver Road in Edgbaston and the reason for this was again linked with access to a Roman Catholic church. Mabel had now chosen the Birmingham Oratory church in preference to St Dunstan's, as it was only a short walk from Oliver Road.

This was the first English community of the Congregation of the Oratory, the order started in Rome by St Philip Neri in the sixteenth century. This community was founded by John Henry Newman in 1848 and moved to the present site on the Hagley Road in 1852, where the community house and temporary church were built. John Henry Newman was made a Cardinal in 1879 and the present church, built in a basilica-style was started in 1903 and completed in 1909.

While still living in Oliver Road, Mabel, Ronald and Hilary became friendly with Father Francis Xavier Morgan, who was the local parish priest, but in 1904 Mabel became ill with diabetes and spent some time in hospital. Back in the early part of the twentieth century many illnesses that today can be controlled or even cured could be fatal and one of the best prescriptions for recovery after an illness was fresh air. So the family moved just out of Birmingham and stayed in Fern Cottage in the grounds of Oratory House in Rednal. Oratory House stands on the wooded slopes of Rednal Hill, part of the Lickey Hills, and was used as a retreat by members of the Oratory community. Fern Cottage and Oratory House still exist today but much of the large grounds have now been built on. The latest housing development to be built there is called Rowan Trees.

The Lickey Hills, made up of Rednal Hill, Beacon Hill, Rose Hill, Crofton Hill and Lickey Warren, must have been a real breath of fresh air with their wooded slopes and carpets of bluebells in the late spring. The views from Beacon Hill would have given them two different worlds to look at, one looking back onto the smoky city, the other onto the rolling fields and farms of Worcestershire, with the Malvern Hills on the distant horizon. The bus and tram services had not yet

38 British Camp or Herefordshire Beacon with its earth ramparts and ditches from the time it was an Iron Age hill fort and, at the top, The Citadel.

39 The winter sun setting behind British Camp.

reached this outer area as they were destined to do just before the First World War. Then the arrival of convenient transport changed the area in character from rural villages to a leisure playground for Birmingham people. (plate 28; p. 81)

But, after a wonderful summer in the woods and fields of the Lickey Hills and the glorious colours of the trees in the autumn, Mabel's diabetes overcame her and she died in November 1904.

Oliver Road was completely redeveloped in the later part of the twentieth century and now only the name lives on.

The Oratory buildings on Hagley Road, Edgbaston, *c.* 1905.

The Oratory church today.

After a short time Ronald, who was twelve, and Hilary, who was ten, returned to Edgbaston to live with their aunt Beatrice Suffield in Stirling Road, a short distance from the Oratory. The house, a Victorian town house of three storeys, at the time would have combined varnished mahogany woodwork and doors, high ceilings and ornate plasterwork in the living rooms and there would have been a bell system for calling the servants. The atmosphere in the house would have seemed quite different from in the same house today. In the daytime, without radios and televisions and the sounds of passing traffic, it would have been quiet and at night there would be the ticking of clocks, clocks chiming the hours and in the evening, when the gaslights were lit, there would be a constant low hissing from the gaslights.

Living on the other side of the road was the widow of the locally famous surgeon Dr Joseph Sampson Gamgee. Dr Gamgee was born in Italy to Scottish parents in 1822 and educated in Europe and was a friend of Joseph Lister and Louis Pasteur in later life. He founded the Birmingham Hospital Saturday Fund in 1873, which helped members with hospital bills as it still does today. He also invented Gamgee tissue, cotton dressing used for dressing wounds, which was used greatly in the First World War and is still in use today.

He died in 1886, but his name lives on as a major character in *The Lord of the Rings*, as Frodo's companion on the quest is Sam Gamgee who also is a ring-bearer for a short time in the book. *Now that he was himself growing old and stiff in the joints, the job was mainly carried on by his youngest son, Sam Gamgee. Both father and son were on very*

The Oratory (Old Church)
Birmingham.

An old view of the interior of the Oratory old church.

friendly terms with Bilbo and Frodo. They lived on the Hill itself, in Number 3 Bagshot Row just below Bag End. (*The Fellowship of the Ring*, A Long-expected Party.) In a strange twist of fate the headquarters of the Birmingham Hospital Saturday Fund moved to a new building in 1975 called Gamgee House at the end of Oliver Road.

At the end of Stirling Road stands a tall chimney: one of many that form a forest of chimneys on the Birmingham skyline. But this is not an ordinary circular brick sort of chimney, but a beautiful Italianate-style red brick one with ornamental cream bricks that was built in 1862. Standing next to the chimney is the boiler house, engine room and workshops of the Edgbaston Water Works that was pumping water day and night to supply water to Birmingham and Aston from bore holes.

This was a busy site at the time when the Tolkien brothers lived in Edgbaston in the early 1900s and there would have been much horse-drawn traffic coming and going from the site. This would have been carrying coal, most likely from the canal a short distance away, to feed the ever-hungry boilers that supplied steam for the beam engines that pumped the water.

The great chimney would sometimes have belched black smoke and the sound of the engines pumping would have been felt and heard. In the engine-house, men would have been oiling the great engine as the connecting rods moved up and down and beams rocked like giant seesaws. The spinning weights of the engine governors would flash in the light as they controlled the speed of the engines. In the boiler-house there would have been rows of boilers supplying steam to the

Above: Hagley Road, Edgbaston just opposite the Plough and Harrow Hotel, *c.* 1905. The Oratory community is visible just behind the horse-drawn bus. Ronald and Hilary would sometimes have travelled by horse-drawn bus into the city centre.

Left: A blue plaque on a modern building at the Five Ways road junction records that Tolkien lived nearby.

Below: Five Ways junction as Ronald Tolkien would have seen it when he travelled to school in the city centre.

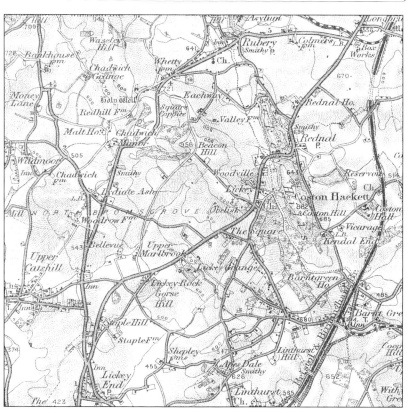

Lickey Hills, *c.* 1900. (Ordnance Survey, Worcestershire sheet X1 NW, Warwickshire X1X NW)

engines, fuelled by stokers with shovels or by mechanical chain grate boiler feeds from coalbunkers above.

One of the architects involved in the design of the waterworks' buildings was John H. Chamberlain who was the architect of Highbury, the grand mansion that Ronald and Hilary had views of from the back of their house in Westfield Road. Chamberlain wanted to put the beauty of nature back into Victorian cities that he felt had been lost during the Industrial Revolution and was also a friend of William Morris the great Pre-Raphaelite visionary and founder of the Arts and Craft movement in the nineteenth century.

A short distance further down the aptly named Waterworks Road, just before the junction of Monument Road, stands a second tower, but this is a true tower in every sense. This beautiful jewel of architecture was built in brick in 1758 for Humphrey Perrott next to his hunting lodge in the ancient enclosed hunting park that went back into the fourteenth century when it was owned by the Lords of Birmingham and was called Parc de Rotton Juxta Birmingham. (plate 29; p. 84)

Oratory House on the side of Rednal Hill.

The quiet village of Rednal in the early years of the twentieth century.

The tower, known as Perrott's Folly, has a spiral staircase of 139 steps with small rooms on each floor and the roof of the tower has a stone-embattled parapet. The height of the tower is 96 feet. There have been many speculations about Perrott's possible reasons for building the tower. Popular ones include providing a vantage point for his daughter to watch him hunting in the park, another so that he could see his sweetheart in a nearby village and yet another so that he could see the far-off village of Belbroughton where his wife was buried. The most likely reason though was just to let him see where the deer were in the park. He entertained

Rednal area showing Fern Cottage and Oratory House.

① Lickey Road going into Birmingham

② Oratory House

③ Fern Cottage

his friends in the sixth-floor room, which still has a domed ceiling and plaster cornices and Rococo, Gothic-framed emblematic designs with roses and acanthus. It must have been hard work for the servant carrying the food and wine up the spiral staircase! In the later part of the nineteenth century the tower became one of the world's first weather stations, under the guidance of the pioneering meteorologist A. Follett Osler.

The two towers are locally believed to be Minas Morgul and Minas Tirith, but Tolkien himself was never clear about which pair of towers *The Two Towers* is named after. *Then the watch up on the walls of*

Fern Cottage as it is today (2006).

One of the stylish plaques on the gates to Fern Cottage recording that the Tolkien family lived there. The plaque shows characters from *The Lord of the Rings*.

Mordor slept, slept, and dark things crept back to Gorgoroth. And on a time evil things came forth, and took Minas Ithil and abode in it, and they made it into a place dread; and it is called Minas Morgal, the Tower of Sorcery. Then Minas Anor was named anew Minas Tirith, the Tower of Guard...(The Fellowship of the Ring, The Council of Elrond)

The Old High Road at the Lickey Hills.

While living in Stirling Road, Ronald would have walked past a Victorian public house on the corner of Monument Road and the Hagley Road as he went to and from school in the centre of Birmingham. That public house is called the Ivy Bush and it was to reappear many years later as the Ivy Bush Tavern in Hobbiton. *He held forth at The Ivy Bush, a small inn on the Bywater road...*(*The Fellowship of the Ring*, A Long-expected Party.)

In 1908 Ronald and Hilary moved from Stirling Road to Duchess Road to live at Mrs Faulkner's house and living there at the time was Edith Bratt, also an orphan, and a romance started to blossom between Ronald and Edith. They most likely would have gone for walks around Edgbaston Reservoir, a short walk from Duchess Road, which in those days was like an inland seaside attraction. It had a bandstand, rowing boats for hire and beaches. (plate 30; p. 85)

Father Francis Morgan frowned on this relationship and he had Hilary and Ronald moved out of Duchess Road and into a house in Highfield Road just over the road from the Oratory. This was the last house in which Ronald was to stay in Birmingham and a Blue Plaque records that he lived there from 1910 to 1911. While living at this house, Father Francis Morgan banned Ronald from carrying on with this relationship and Edith moved away from Birmingham to live in Cheltenham. But before Edith left Birmingham she and Ronald had a chance meeting one lunchtime in Moseley Village in the Prince of Wales public house.

The tale now moves away from the Birmingham area, as Ronald went to Oxford University and visited parts of Europe, but he returned

One of the fine walks on the Lickey Hills, *c.* 1910.

An old view of Bilberry Hill at the Lickey Hills.

to Edgbaston at Christmas to be in a play at his old school King Edward's in the city centre. One would imagine that he stayed with Hilary in Highfield Road at this time.

At the age of twenty-one, while still at Oxford University, he made contact again with Edith, who was about to get married to someone else and the contact restarted their romance. Ronald finished at Oxford in the summer of 1915, by which time the war was raging in

Above: Part of Bilberry Hill today.

Left: Aunt Beatrice Suffield's house in Stirling Road as it is today. The Tolkien brothers lived in the attic rooms at the top of the house, which at the time might otherwise have been allocated to the servants.

Europe and he joined the Lancashire Fusiliers and went to fight. He and Edith were eventually married in the spring of 1916.

The couple returned to Birmingham in the June of 1916 and stayed at the Plough and Harrow Hotel just over the road from the Oratory

Left: A plaque on the Repertory Theatre in the city centre, recording the life and work of J. Sampson Gamgee.

Below: The entrance to Gamgee House, home of the Birmingham Hospital Saturday Fund.

and stopped for one night only. Ronald was most likely on embarkation leave, as he was shortly to go the Western Front and it would be nice to think that they were returning to the places of their childhood sweetheart days. They stayed in room 116 in the Plough and Harrow, where there is also now a Blue Plaque recording their short stay.

Above: Edgbaston Water Works looking much as it would have done in Tolkien's time here. (courtesy Severn Trent Water Ltd)

Right: The Edgbaston Water Works chimney and other buildings that have survived from the 1860s.

The type of boilerhouse that would have supplied steam to the pumping engine at the waterworks.

The steamy atmosphere around a preserved steam engine.

The doorway into Perrott's Folly leading to the 139-step spiral staircase.

The Ivy Bush public house on the Hagley Road today. Its exterior has changed little since Ronald Tolkien passed it on his way to school.

The Hagley Road shops just below the Ivy Bush public house, *c*. 1905.

Duchess Road, Edgbaston in around 1910.

The bandstand and boathouse at Edgbaston Reservoir.

Edgbaston Reservoir with beach, hire boats and a forest of chimneys beyond the dam, *c.* 1905.

The Walk, Edgbaston Reservoir, *c.* 1910. Perhaps Ronald and Edith went court-
ing along this tree-lined walk.

Above: The view along Highfield
Road as the Tolkien brothers would
have known it.

Left: The plaque recording that
Tolkien lived for a short period in
Highfield Road.

Above: A modern view of the house in Highfield Road where the Tolkien brothers lived.

Left: The Prince of Wales public house in Moseley Village today.

Plough and Harrow Hotel viewed from the end of Highfield Road, *c.* 1910.

The Plough and Harrow Hotel today. Its appearance has changed little since Edith and Ronald stayed there in 1916.

Right: St Mary Immaculate church in Warwick, a short distance from Warwick Castle, where Ronald and Edith were married.

Below: Warwick Castle.

Above: Symbols of a plough and harrow on a gable end of the Plough and Harrow Hotel recalling its rural past.

Left: A plaque on the Plough and Harrow Hotel recording Ronald and Edith's stay.

Chapter 8

The Great Tower

During the period that Ronald and Hilary were living in Edgbaston another strange tower was slowly growing skyward on the horizon which, when completed, would be 315 feet high. The tower is known as the Chamberlain Tower after Joseph Chamberlain who created Birmingham University from a number of city colleges. The tower, locally nick-named Old Joe, appeared mysteriously to be rising without visible means as it was built from the inside with no exterior scaffolding.

The tower was designed by Sir Aston Webb and is based on the Mangia Tower in Siena. It cost around £25,000, a sum of money that could have financed, it was pointed out at the time, a Chair in one of the University faculties and it was for a long time considered to be a bit of a white elephant. Today it is an important landmark on the Birmingham skyline and at night it can still be seen from many locations, with the illuminated clock faces becoming like eyes although sadly they are not red or yellow: *But suddenly the Mirror went altogether dark, as dark as if a hole had opened in the world of sight, and Frodo looked into emptiness. In the black abyss there appeared a single Eye that slowly grew, until it filled nearly all the Mirror... The Eye was rimmed with fire, but was itself glazed, yellow as a cat's, watchful and intent.* (*The Fellowship of the Ring*, The Mirror of Galadriel.) (plate 31; p. 85)

The clock tower became useful in 1940 and started to 'see' in new ways, because it was used for experiments on radar by Sir Mark Oliphant. In one of the battles in *The Two Towers* large elephants are used by the Haradrim as beasts of war and these are called Oliphaunts. This could be a strange coincidence – but who can tell today? *Sam stood up, putting his hands behind his back (as he always did when 'speaking poetry'), and began: ...*

...I make the earth shake,
As I tramp through the grass;
Trees crack as I pass.

A modern view of the clock tower and some of the original university buildings.

The University of Birmingham in Edgbaston soon after its construction in the early years of the twentieth century.

With horns in my mouth
I walk in the South,
Flapping big ears.
Beyond count of years
I stump round and round,
Never lie on the ground,
Not ever to die.
Oliphaunt am I,
Biggest of all, ...
(*The Two Towers*, The Black Gate is Closed.)

Birmingham University was to play a role in Tolkien's life in 1916. At the start of the First World War the University Great Hall was turned into a 520-bed hospital called the 1st Southern Military Hospital. In 1915 more buildings were being used and the number of beds went up to 1,000. Also within the area schools and grand houses, such as Highbury, were also being turned into hospitals to cope with the rising number of casualties from the war. By the summer of 1916 the university hospital had a total of 1,570 beds. Wounded soldiers were transported by train to Birmingham and then to Selly Oak station goods yard. They were then transferred to the hospital in two-wheeled trailer ambulances, towed by locally owned private cars fitted with tow bars. A local man, Mr E. Tailby, designed these special trailers.

Tolkien was brought to the hospital in November 1916 suffering from trench fever. He stayed in hospital for around six weeks,

Birmingham University Great Hall used as a huge ward in the 1st Southern Military Hospital with sunlight shining through the arched window. This must have been a strange place to wake up in. Tolkien was brought here after suffering Trench Fever in the First World War.

before going to Great Haywood to convalesce. A postcard from the 1st Southern Military Hospital, bearing a picture of the university on the front, was sent by a relative of one of its patients which sums up the horrors of the times: *Just to let you know that Eddie is a lot better. He's quite bright considering his condition. We have lodgings close by and can visit often.*

Tolkien would also have seen and been reminded of the Tower when he returned in later years to Birmingham for school reunions as his old school King Edward VI had moved to new buildings just across the road from the university. (plates 32, 33; pp 88)

The central dome at Birmingham University. Many other buildings were used as hospital wards and a total of 67,000 patients were treated at the 1st Southern Military Hospital by the end of the First World War.

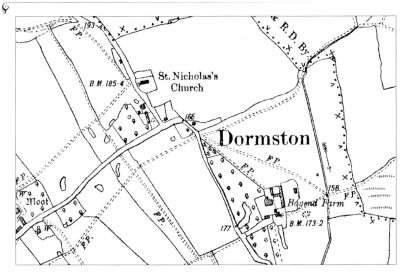

Dormston, 1905. Bagend Farm is shown on the right-hand side of the map spelt as one word, but it appears as two words on older maps. (Ordnance Survey, Worcestershire sheet XXX SW)

Ashton-Under-Hill in Worcestershire.

Chapter 9

Worcestershire

After the First World War both of the Tolkien brothers moved away from the Birmingham area. Hilary moved to Worcestershire and bought a smallholding and orchard. Their Aunt Jane also moved to Worcestershire and rented a farm on the edge of the small village of Dormston – the farm on old maps is called Bag End. It is still there today, but has changed its name to Dormston Manor and is a private house with no access to the public. The farm and outbuildings are timber-framed and could date back to the Tudor period. (plate 35; p. 92)

The small church of St Nicholas, a short walk from Bag End, has a square, timber-framed tower at one end of the building that looks as if it has come straight from Middle-earth. These towers are a vernacular tradition in Worcestershire and there are at least four such church towers in the area. (plate 37; p. 93)

The old maps of this area read like places and characters from Middle-earth, with two Underhills, Barrows Field, Brandon Brook, Hollowfields Farm, Dragon Farm, The Bird in the Hand public house and Throckmorton, most likely Frogmorton in the book.

The local legend of Dragon Farm is a wonderful tale that tells of two dragons living a long time ago in an age when other creatures such as wyvern, cockatrice, firedrakes, griffons and gigantic serpents were also alive. The farmer at Dragon Farm was losing sheep from his flock, so he went to see the Rangers, Woodwards and Verderers in Feckenham Forest and they told him that no sheep were straying into the forest and there was no evidence of them being eaten by wolves in the pastures that they grazed.

The farmer went to see a holy man who told him to watch and pray and he put his shepherd on guard at night over the flock. The next night, the shepherd came to the farmer and told him that two dragons were taking the lambs and vanishing with them into a huge oak tree. The farmer shot the dragons and when they went into the oak tree they found that it was hollow inside and the space was so large that

Morton Underhill is a small farming hamlet close to Bag End.

Throckmorton, a village close to Bag End.

there would have been room to turn a coach around within the tree. The three Hobbits on their way to Crickhollow did have a meal in a large hollow tree – coincidence? *Not far from the road-meeting they came on the huge hulk of a tree: it was still alive and had leaves on the small branches that it had put out round the broken stumps of its long-fallen limbs; but it was hollow, and could be entered by a great crack on the side away from the road. The Hobbits crept inside, and sat there upon a floor of old leaves and decayed wood.* (*The Fellowship of the Ring*, Three is Company.)

Inkberrow and Dormston, the two villages close to Bag End, are full of wonderful buildings that look as if they could have come straight from Middle-earth. There are cottages with stone or brick chimneys built at one end of the cottage and from the narrow lanes timber-framed houses and barns can be seen in this still truly rural landscape.

As you round the corner from Bag End on a clear day, a long range of often misty-looking hills comes into view, these are the Malvern Hills – could they be the origin of the Misty Mountains in *The Lord of the Rings*? *Gandalf fell silent, gazing eastward from the porch to the far peaks of the Misty Mountains, at whose great roots the peril of the world had so long lain hidden. He sighed.* (*The Fellowship of the Ring*, The Council of Elrond.) (plate 36; p. 92)

The Malvern Hills would have been fiery mountains 600 million years ago, a long time before Tolkien saw them, but they do have a Shire Ditch running through them that is the border between Worcestershire and Herefordshire.

The Malvern Hills have a history of settlement going back thousands of years and evidence for this can still be seen today at the sites of two Iron Age hill forts, British Camp and Midsummer Camp. Tolkien disliked the influences on the English language of the Norman invasion and the Normans left their mark at the top of British Camp when they built The Citadel on top of it. (plates 38, 39; pp 96)

A dragon carving from Bells Farm in south Birmingham.

Dragon Farm today, viewed from the lane.

Worcestershire Beacon: the highest point on the Malvern Hills at 425 metres above sea level. From an old postcard.

A cottage with thatched roof, large brick chimney and timber-framed buildings in Inkberrow.

The Malvern Hills from the British Camp.

The Malvern Hills seen from the Iron Age fort, or British Camp, from an old postcard.

The Malvern Hills - Ivy Scar on a snowy winter's day.

Chapter 10

The Story Moves On

Now the story moves away from the Birmingham area to other parts of England including Staffordshire, Leeds, Oxford and other places. Ronald did return to Birmingham a number of times but in 1933 he came with his children to show them his own childhood haunts, and found that much had been built over and a suburb called Hall Green had spread across the farms and fields of his childhood. Even Sarehole Farm had changed and had become a petrol station.

Today time and trees have mellowed Hall Green and it has become one of Birmingham's leafy suburbs and many of the old places have survived to this day, as we have seen, and are treasured by the people who live there.

In April 1944 Ronald returned to Birmingham for a school reunion and went to visit the old school site in New Street and was not very impressed with the building that had replaced it, King Edward House. *... I then strolled about my 'home town' for a bit. Except for one patch of ghastly wreckage (opp. My old school's site) it does not look much damaged: not by the enemy. The chief damage has been the growth of great flat featureless modern buildings. The worst of all is the ghastly multiple-site erection on the old site. I couldn't stand much of that or the ghosts that rose from the pavements; so I caught a tram...* (*The Letters of J.R.R. Tolkien*, Letter 58.)

Once again Birmingham had stirred his imagination in the writing of *The Lord of the Rings.* The vision of the ghosts rising from the pavement broke his writing block and he rapidly wrote the chapters 'The Passage of the Marches' and 'The Black Gate is Closed' in *The Two Towers.* Both these chapters draw heavily on his experiences in the Battle of the Somme with water-filled shell holes and blasted chalk landscapes.

Finally, having searched for many of the local places that relate to Tolkien and *The Lord of the Rings*, I failed to find a representation for The Prancing Pony in the area. Well, almost: I did find a public house

Robin Hood Lane in Hall Green was much changed when Tolkien returned to Birmingham. It has changed still further and now has a massive six-road traffic island at one end of it.

The Stratford Road approaching Robin Hood Island as it looked in the 1930s.

called the Prancing Pony at the north end of the Malvern Hills, but then found that the landlord had renamed it thus in 2001 when the first film came out.

But one day while visiting Oxford I was taken to the White Horse public house for lunch; this must be one of the smallest public houses in England. It is completely surrounded by the Tardis-like Blackwells

Above: King Edward's House, the very stylish and imposing building erected on the old school site.

Left: The sign outside the White Horse public house in Oxford. The White Horse does look like a prancing pony.

bookshop and was full of academic-looking men having a drink and lunch. Well, Tolkien and C.S. Lewis apparently went there years ago for a drink and Tolkien would read chapters of *The Lord of the Rings* to Lewis. One chapter in *The Lord of the Rings* is called 'At The Sign of the Prancing Pony' and the pub sign outside today does look very much like a prancing pony!

Minworth Greases, one of the two timber-framed buildings at Selly manor Museum.

Places to Visit

The following is a list of places that have been featured in this book: some are open to the public but many others are not. Private homes featured in the book, when illustrated here, were all photographed from the public highway. If you are visiting any of these please respect the privacy of the owners, don't trespass on their land and please don't do anything else that might annoy or inconvenience them.

For the following public attractions I suggest checking opening times and cost of entrance before setting out as these may have changed since the time of writing. I have included also some sources of old maps that may be useful.

Avoncroft Museum of Historic Buildings Stoke Heath Bromsgrove Worcestershire B60 4JR Web site www.avoncroft.org.uk Many interesting buildings including an iron church.
Blakesley Hall Blakesley Road Yardley Birmingham B25 8RN Website: www.birminghamheritage.org.uk/blakesley.htm The dragon carving for Bells Farm is on display here.
Barber Institute of Fine Arts University of Birmingham Edgbaston Birmingham B15 2TS Website: www.barber.org.uk A wonderful art gallery with great views of the university clock tower.

Bells Farm Centre
Bells Farm Close
Birmingham B14 5QP
Website: www.birminghamheritage.org.uk/bllsfrm.htm
A seventeenth-century timber-framed farmhouse.

Birmingham Oratory
141 Hagley Road
Edgbaston
Birmingham B16 8UE
Website: www.birmingham-oratory.org.uk
Close by are the Plough and Harrow, Ivy Bush and The Two Towers (Perrott's
    Folly and Edgbaston Water Works): neither of the towers is open to the
    public but can be viewed from the pavement.

The Ironbridge Gorge Museums
Coach Road
Coalbrookdale
Shropshire TF8 7DQ
Website: www.ironbridge.org.uk
Here you can find a working steam engine most of the time plus some
    Victorian shops.

Lickey Hills Country Park
The Visitor Centre
Warren Lane
Rednal
Birmingham B45 8ER
Website: www.birmingham.gov.uk/lickeyhills.bcc
Great walks and wonderful bluebell woods in the spring.

Maps
Historical Mapping
Romsey Road
Maybush
Southampton, SO15 4GU
Website: www.ordnancesurvey.co.uk

The Map Shop
15 High Street
Upton Upon Severn
Worcestershire, WR8 0HJ
Website: www.themapshop.co.uk

Mr Alan Godfrey
Prospect Business Park
Leadgate, Consett, DH8 7PW
Web site www.alangodfreymaps.co.uk

Museum of Welsh Life
St Fagans
Cardiff CF5 6XB
Website: www.nmgw.ac.uk/www.php/mwl
Welsh coal trucks can be seen here.

Sarehole Mill
Cole Bank Road
Hall Green
Birmingham B13 0BD
Website: www.birmingham.gov.uk/sarehole.bcc

Selly Manor Museum
Sycamore Road
Bournville
Website: www.bvt.org.uk/sellymanor
Two wonderful timber-framed buildings that look as if they were moved here
    from Bree in the film.

The Shire Country Park, Sarehole Mill
Website www.birmingham.gov.uk/shirecountrypark

Bibliography

Birmingham Pals, Terry Carter, (Barnsley: Pen & Sword 1997)

Farmer Giles of Ham: J.R.R. Tolkien, (Harper Collins Publishers 1993)

Hall Green, The Archive Photograph Series, Michael Byrne (Chalford Publishing 1996)

J.R.R. Tolkien A Biography, Humphrey Carpenter (Unwin Paperbacks 1978)

Journeys of Frodo, Barbara Strachey (Harper Collins Publishers 1981)

Kelly's Director of Birmingham (with its suburbs) and *Smethwick*, (Kelly's Directories Ltd 1892 to 1946)

More About Inkberrow, R. Hunt and R. Jackson, (private publication 1976)

Roverandom, J.R.R. Tolkien, (Harper Collins Publishers 1998)

Smith of Wootton Major, J.R.R. Tolkien, (Unwin Hyman Ltd 1990)

The Atlas of Middle-earth, Kaven Wynn Fonstad, (Harper Collins Publishers 1994)

The Cole Valley South (The Millstream Way), John Morris Jones (Published by the River Cole and Chinn Brook Conservation Group 1989)

The Complete Guide to Middle-Earth, Robert Foster, (Unwin Paperbacks 1978)

The Grange, King's Heath, S.A. Budd (Occasional Paper No.1 King's Heath Local History Society 1987)

The Hobbit, J.R.R. Tolkien (Unwin Books 1967)

The Letters of J.R.R. Tolkien, Edited by Humphrey Carpenter with the assistance of Christopher Tolkien, (Unwin Paperbacks 1990)

The Lord of the Rings, J.R.R. Tolkien, (George Allen & Unwin Ltd 1968)

The Man Who Planted Trees, Jean Giono, (The Harvill Press 1995)

The Real Middle Earth, Brian Bates, (Pan Books 2003)

The Road to Middle-Earth, Tom Shippey (Grafton 1992)

The Tolkien Family Album, John & Priscilla Tolkien, (Harper Collins Publishers 1992)

Tolkien, a Biography, Michael White (Little Brown & Co. 2001)

Tolkien and the Great War, John Garth, (Harper Collins Publishers 2004)

'Tolkien's Shire', John Ezard, (*Weekend Guardian* December 28/29 1991)

Index